FOREST BOOKS

POET? CRIMINAL? MADMAN?

EWA LIPSKA was born on 8 October 1945, in Kraków, Poland. She won praise for her poetry in her teens. She studied art history and painting at the Kraków Academy of Fine Arts but continued to write poetry and has published verse, drama and prose regularly ever since her influential first collection appeared in 1967.

In 1970 she became poetry editor of the leading publishing house Wydawnictwo Literackie. In 1973 she received the Kościelski Fund Award (Geneva). This was followed by an invitation from the University of Iowa to work in the USA (1975–6). In 1979 she received the Robert Graves PEN Club Award. She co-founded the literary monthly *Pismo* and edited it from 1981–3. Her 1985 collection *Przechowalnia ciemności* (The Storeroom of Darkness) was published by the underground Warsaw Independent Poets' and Artists' Publishing House.

She has travelled widely and has been translated into Croatian, Czech, Danish, Dutch, English, French, German, Hungarian, Norwegian, Serbian, Swedish and other languages. In 1990 she became Poland's cultural representative in Vienna.

BARBARA PLEBANEK grew up in Poland. She translated poetry and prose and her work has been published in *Poetry Review*, *The Rialto*, *Literatura na Świecie* and *New Theatre Quarterly*. She now lives in London with her daughter and practises traditional Chinese medicine.

TONY HOWARD has written widely on Polish theatre. His plays include *A Short Sharp Shock*, written with Howard Brenton (Stratford East and Royal Court Theatre).

Ewa Lipska

Poet?
Criminal?
Madman?

Poems
by

Ewa
Lipska

FOREST
BOOKS
London & Boston

Introduction by Adam Czerniawski
Translated by Barbara Plebanek & Tony Howard

Published by
FOREST BOOKS

20 Forest View, Chingford, London E4 7AY, U.K.
61 Lincoln Road, Wayland, MA 01778, U.S.A.

FIRST PUBLISHED 1991

Typeset in Great Britain by Cover to Cover, Cambridge
Printed in Great Britain by BPCC Wheatons Ltd, Exeter

Original poems © Ewa Lipska
Introduction © Adam Czerniawski
Translations © Barbara Plebanek and Tony Howard
Cover Design © Ian Evans

ISBN 1 85610 011 1

British Library Cataloguing-in-Publication Data
A catalogue record for this book is
available from the British Library

Library of Congress Catalog Card No:
91–72165

Forest Books gratefully acknowledges financial support for this
volume from the Arts Council of Great Britain

These translations are for
Stefania, Maire, Kaya

Contents

Note:

The dates accompanying the translations indicate the year in
which the original Polish volume appeared. Poems dated 1991 are
new pieces, unpublished in book form in Poland at the time of
going to press.

Introduction

For decades the map of twentieth-century Polish poetry, as made available to the English-language reader, was totally blank. Some thirty years ago the first two points of reference appeared: the poetry of Tadeusz Różewicz and Zbigniew Herbert. These two poets were born in the twenties; they were then joined by their elders Czesław Miłosz (born 1911) and Aleksander Wat (1900–67), and most recently by a contemporary, Wisława Szymborska. In the interest of genealogical symmetry, we should next expect a thirties poet to make an appearance. Perhaps Bogdan Czaykowski will be the one. Meanwhile, we have skipped a generation. We have a substantial volume of Ewa Lipska's poems.

What is new and remarkable about Lipska? She was born in 1945 and that already is remarkable, for it sets her apart from her elders who have all experienced World War II. In a youthful poem she observes ironically:

> We – the postwar generation wide open
> in perfectly physical comfort
> read Sartre and phone books.
>
> [. . . .]
>
> We envy those
> who went through the war
> in cavalry boots.

She was also therefore among the first to be born in the Polish People's Republic. The hostility towards the communist system, which she and other writers of her generation had in time developed, has therefore a special significance: the carefully organised ideological indoctrination policy of the government had failed to retain the loyalty of impressionable young minds. She remarks:

Poet? Criminal? Madman?

The citizen of a small country
Thoughtlessly born on the edge of Europe
is called up to contemplate freedom.

New and fresh too is Lipska's poetic voice, particularly so
when seen in the context of these other poetic voices. Wat,
Miłosz, Różewicz, Szymborska and Herbert are, on the
whole, content to express their poetry in apparently straightforward conventional sentences. For example Wat writes:

She swept the room with a casually professional look,
sized up two old men bent over their dominoes
and hesitated suddenly when meeting my eyes –

Miłosz writes:

Between her and me there was a table, on the table a glass.
The rough skin of her elbows touched the shining surface
Where the shadow of her armpit was reflected.

Herbert writes:

She practiced woman's oldest profession
She was mourned briefly but sincerely by the soldiers
of the Third Legion
and a certain aged officer

Różewicz writes:

young
radiant
women
appeared
under a granite colonnade
in ballroom gowns

Szymborksa writes:

Her eyes are, as required, now deep blue, now grey,
black, sparkling, unaccountably filled with tears.

But Lipska writes:

x

A language failure has occurred nationwide.

[. . . .]

Drowned meanings have sunk to the bottom.
Words have got out of order.

For Lipska this failure is not a temporary breakdown. Judging by the recurring references in her poetry to this phenomenon, it seems a permanent state of affairs. In her experience 'Language melts in sunlight' and 'Sense wandered off'. Not surprising therefore that:

As we tried to talk to each other
it turned out
we had different tongues

Thus, unlike her elders,* she is deeply self-conscious about language. She discovers that 'speech constrains us' and that language 'is ripe for cruelty and treason', and no wonder, given that so much of it is 'the official state language'. Consequently, the poets I have cited all have a much greater faith in the normality of reality than Lipska has. She is here the irrationalist amongst rationalists. It's a dangerous situation to be in, as Lipska herself realises:

Tell me,   do you think mankind's insane?
Insane,   incomprehensible,   aren't they the same?

While their 'I's are often hidden behind masks, like Herbert's Pan Cogito or Szymborska's array of fictional and historical characters, who all confidently address the world at large, most of Lipska's poems are couched in the form of personal confessions, though, as usual in such instances, it would be risky to treat them as straightforward autobiography. This personal perspective does however tie up with her distrust of language, and therefore of communication. Her 'I' finds it

---

* Nothing is ever simple in these matters. In his youth Wat did experiment with language quite drastically; while Tymoteusz Karpowicz (born 1921) and Miron Białoszewski (1922–83) proved even more radical in this respect. But what sets Lipska apart is her scepticism. They pushed their language games to the limits only in the unquestioning belief that they had an understanding audience, however small.

Poet? Criminal? Madman?

difficult to make contact with the outside world. Maybe that is
why what her eye (or 'I') sees is often so startling and strange:

> The child was born abnormal.
> A volcano cried out from its mouth
> and froze in the air.
> [. . . .]
> You can only look at the child when it's asleep.
> Then it looks like an angel
> that fell on its head.

This is the stuff that dreams are made of; except that in
Lipska's case it is very much the stuff out of which what we
would call 'reality' is made. When her friend and – some say –
her mentor, Wisława Szymborksa, writes a dream-poem, she
gives us due warning. And so in a poem entitled plainly 'In
praise of dreams', she feels free to say that she paints like
Vermeer, has seen two suns and 'managed to discover
Atlantis'. But even Szymborska's dreams are less disturbing
than Lipska's reality where, for example, we are told that:

> We are all alike
> and look like shares falling
> or a lethal telegram

If Dr Johnson is right that metaphors are ideas yoked together
by violence, then these are metaphors with a vengeance.

Perhaps only Różewicz records at times a somewhat similarly deranged reality. But interestingly, while he is certainly
a much more thorough sceptic than she is, doubting many
things in the sphere of ethics and art, including the language
of poetry, he has not raised doubts about language simply as
a means of talking to others, and therefore about the nature
and reality of the world. But both poets also feel at home in
related paradoxical situations. Różewicz continues to write
poems about poems he doesn't wish to or can't write; Lipska,
despite the persistent language failures she encounters, carries
on writing with exuberance, energy and wit.

Adam Czerniawski

Translators' Preface

Ewa Lipska has been translated world-wide. Her remarkable adaptability may be due to the strong visual
qualities of her poems. Sometimes they resemble a still life ('I
work here', 'Good-bye everyone', 'Lunar eclipse'), sometimes
dramatic scenes ('Confessions of a courtesan', 'Tourist group',
'Class 1'), and it is often possible to feel the artist's brush
strokes being transformed into words. Often she performs
this manoeuvre by employing everyday language, then
breaking it down and fusing the fragments with a new
unexpected nucleus:

> . . . fawning linguists
> putting the language in curlers.

> ('From the Series: Great power-failures (I)')

> Someone else had crime on the tip of his tongue.

> ('No way out')

Thus she creates two simultaneous worlds of meaning: the
implied standard world collides with the newly created one,
generating an explosion of energy within the poem. An
Einsteinian universe. 'Great power-failures' is a clinical
example of the technique, but nearly every poem demonst-
rates this powerful tension between what is in the text and
what the reader visualizes through linguistic association:

Poet? Criminal? Madman?

> . . . her child . . .
> who has burst a glass into tears.

('Anxiety')

> On the desk a canned poem.

('I work here')

> The first kept adjusting my thoughts and collars.

('Tourist group')

> far too everything.

('Last words')

> Why doesn't Homer know the structure of the atom
> shutting his eyes to whatever's on the board?

('Class 1')

> *I'm off for a rest*
> *in the Bermuda Triangle.*

('To Marianna Büttrich')

So Lipska can be specific and universal, down-to-earth and abstract at the same time. Her concreteness creates a sense of immediacy, as seen in her so-called political poems (for instance, 'The last caretaker'). But by playing her phrase-breaking game she brings out a transcendental element which carries her meaning far beyond the immediate political allusions.

Lipska is often said to be preoccupied with death in her writing. As a young woman she fought a battle for life. Consequently, she seems neither infatuated with life nor paranoid about death. She appears to be liaising between the two realms, treating them as inseperable and mutually dependent. She does that by constantly mixing their colours on the imaginary canvas and colliding their vocabularies on paper:

xiv

Why don't you try and do something human?
Don't be posthumous.

('Why don't you try and do something human? . . .')

You set out for San Francisco
and I'm dying.

('Two Letters')

In 'Dawn' it is the selfishness of life as much as the cruelty of
death that hurts. Not surprisingly, then, spirits emerge from
those poems, earth-bound – not romantic – ghosts. They
behave exactly like the living ('From a journey'). Similarly,
she sees love and hate as two aspects of the same drive:

'They're so in love that from that hate . . .'

('They')

This is a kind of wisdom that cannot be expressed other than
through paradox. Subtle irony. No overt enthusiasms. No
simplistic judgement.

Poetry like this puts us in touch with the shadow line that
we try so desperately to avoid in life. Not surprisingly, Lipska
sees her writing as a form of psychotherapy. Indeed, even the
poems about mediocrity ('So what if he's mediocre? . . .', 'I
didn't become a great statesman . . .', 'Voice') are liberating,
often through gentle humour. They expose the fact that
evading confrontation in life leaves the individual empty.
Perhaps this is why the poet never spares us linguistic
confrontation.

It is usually in the last couple of verses that Lipska
perplexes the reader and tests his or her faith in the poem;
through enigmatic lines which, once contemplated, may
open up a mystery.

In an empty restaurant
the waiter serves me
a hawk's eye.

('A hawk's eye')

Poet? Criminal? Madman?

And they alone already knew
that one step forward is simply death
and one step back merely murder.

('No way out')

In these listless times
when the black swan in your eye
means ill fortune.

('Confessions of a courtesan')

In preparing this volume the translators tried to meet the
task of transferring the phrase-breaking technique from the
Polish into English in order to preserve this energizing
friction between the verbal and the pictorial worlds in
Lipska's poetry.

This collection comes after Ewa Lipska's tour of Britain in
1990. An early English language edition, *Such Times*, appeared in Canada (translated by John Robert Colombo and
Wacław Iwaniuk, Hounslow Press, Toronto, 1981). Several
translations by Magnus Krynski were published in *The Polish
Review* in 1980. Susan Bassnett's and Piotr Kuchiwczak's
Ariadne's Thread: Polish Women Poets (Forest Books, London,
1988), contains eight poems by Lipska. Wherever possible we
referred to the existing English language versions, and in a
few places we are indebted to their authors.

Earlier versions of some of these translations have ap-
peared in *Poetry Review, The Rialto* and *The Mature Laurel:
Essays on Modern Polish Poetry* (ed. Adam Czerniawski, Seren
Books, 1991).

Work on this edition has been greatly assisted by the
hospitality of the British Centre for Literary Translation,
University of East Anglia, and particularly by the encourage-
ment and advice of Adam Czerniawski. We owe a special
debt to Paul Merchant, who, with his skill and sensitivity to
poetic form, helped with the final revision. Above all, we
must thank Ewa Lipska.

Barbara Plebanek & Tony Howard

1
We

Oko jastrzębia

Przeżyłem 75 lat
a zapamiętałem tylko jedną godzinę
w miasteczku Vejer de la Frontera
podczas której nie działo się nic oprócz życia.
Przeczytałem tysiące książek
a zapamiętałem tylko jedno zdanie:
'Tu pytam czy to nie szaleństwo
z trwogi przed śmiercią umierać?'
Podziwiałem wielkich malarzy
a przed oczami długi kondukt dymu
na wyblakłej tapecie nieba.
Ucichły wielkie orkiestry.
Z nieszczelnego zegarka
ulatnia się czas.
Coraz częściej zamyślam się nad niczym.
W pustej restauracji
kelner podaje mi
oko jastrzębia.

Testament

Po śmierci Boga
otworzymy testament
aby dowiedzieć się
do kogo należy świat
i
ta wielka łapka
na ludzi.

A hawk's eye

I've been alive for 75 years
yet I only remember one hour
in the little town Vejer de la Frontera
during which nothing happened but life.
I've read thousands of books
yet I only remember one sentence:
'I now ask: is it not madness
to die from the terror of death?'
I've admired great painters
yet before my eyes is a long cortège of smoke
on bleached sky wallpaper.
Great orchestras have hushed.
From the unproofed watch
time's leaking.
More and more I muse over nothing.
In an empty restaurant
the waiter serves me
a hawk's eye.

(1990)

The will

When God's dead
we'll read the will
to find out
who owns the world
and
that great
mantrap.

(1974)

I work here

I work here. In the East of Europe.
Surrounded by dogs. Small and awkward.
By people sad or drunk.
Or tragic like August Strindberg's.
On the desk a canned poem.
A glove.   Letters.   In the window – ink.
At the room's centre – an armchair
from Tutenkhamun's tomb.
The paper is still breathing
but heavily. With nitroglicerine.
My time.   My body.   My life.
Everything disposable
just like a paper dress or a napkin.
The only certain thing is the shadow in the corner of the room.
A black taxi
growing with the years.

(1990)

We

We – the postwar generation wide open –
in perfect physical comfort
read Sartre and phone books.
We analyse every earthquake in detail.
We. The postwar generation grown in peaceful flower pots.
Deduced from irrefutable statistics.
Unheard in the clatter of the beginning.
Suffering from insomnia, moth-like.
Called up to concentrate.

Rusted doors open onto our days.
Stairs that outlived the canary breeder.
A waterfall of steps. A funeral with an orchestra. And the
                              scream of hurled saucepans.

We descend slowly. Very slowly. Solemn as wood.
It could be seven in the morning. The day ripens too exactly
and sometimes tastes of rotten apple.
All kinds of people run out violently.
Down the stairs.   Through gates.   From hotels.
                              Out of the mouth.   Here and there.
Tenants of the world, insane to the bone.
They curse. They stop at the prepaid parking lot.

We envy those
who went through the war
in cavalry boots.
We envy
the nights sparingly bit by bit
shared amongst tired helmets.
Shots speeding to the mouth like fireworks.
The vulgar melodramas of hair's-breadth escapes.

That dawn
fear was tarred and feathered
and bullets swept up.
Though faces still shuddered steaming hot

5

a fanfare glued together the liberation and the ruins
and wounded walls stood up for the anthem.
People clapped hands to freedom. Gates opened.
In the gates women gave birth:
To us.   How festive.   Called up well before dawn.
Immune to the body. Shaken free of the weapons' crash.

Our birth was in honour of – the dead.
And the bullet-ridden memory is borne
by us.

(1967)

The House of Quiet Youth

At the protest rental centre
the canteen's open.

A red wine lake
flows by the windows.

Risking history
you can swim in it.

Hurrah doesn't always
signal victory here.

Most of all they like
the national gambit.

In the gaming rooms
they win great defeats.

Some pick wild strawberries
and material evidence.

Under a full sail of bedclothes
they cruise off into sleep.

Others stare at the door blankly
as though rescue might come that way.

Some think of another country overhead
this place is too hot for them.

The House of Quiet Youth
is grey as a dove.

(1978)

From the dreambook

If you dream about power
watch your mouth
for a week.

(1978)

The day of the living

On the day of the living
the dead visit the living's graves
– switch on the neon
and dig round the chrysanthemum aerials
on the roofs of multi-storey
centrally heated tombs.

Afterwards
they go down by lift
to their everyday work
to death.

(1974)

Honey

This honey comes from an empire.
The sun
rises over the empire.
Little blue uniforms
buzz.

Fifteen thousand workers
set out
for three hundred thousand flowers.

In the empire the fight for the throne continues.
Sting after sting
falls.

The drones stick up posters:
For one kilogram of honey
twenty thousand flights.

Those
who managed to flee the empire
live in solitude in clover blossoms.
Sometimes they stop at exotic hotels.
Squat on prime ministers' sleeves.
Join the last supper in a Milan monastery.

Sometimes they perish
in history textbooks
slammed shut.

Sometimes
in a pale jar of honey
the liquid empire of greed.

(1982)

From the series:
Great power-failures (I)

A language failure has occurred nationwide.
Since the small hours language engineers
have been trying to hold back floods of words.
Drowned meanings have sunk to the bottom.
Words have got out of order.
Clauses have become dependent
on the generals of one corpse
in the sign of Scorpio the parrot
employed to speak the slogans
of fawning linguists
putting the language in curlers.
Coiffured speech
vanished in cascading streams.
There have been rumours of a phoneme revaluation.
Dams of podia have been put up in panic.
Megaphones have been hung from the trees.
The armoured cars drove in
with word-jugglers.
But language weakened. At the end of its tether.
An aphasia epidemic began to spread.
Sense got lost
in the first flowering
of suspicions and strawberries.
Manipulators worked round the clock.
The thread snapped.
Now nothing hung in newspapers but
black suits of type.
Formlessness spilled from mouths.
Whispers and confessions perished.
Somebody still tried to rise to an answer
but it was drowned in dazzling flood-lights.
Earth moved.
The first geraniums fell.
Torrential rain washed out ditched allusions
scraps of dictionaries and maps.

Several weeks later
a survivor
interviews himself:
Time to make a new start
it's best to begin by mimicking birds
he says
dragging with difficulty out of his mouth
the grinding sounds of meaning.

Later still:
the first commands start to ring out
podia return
the alphabet stretches
with more and more letters.
Day shrinks.

(1985)

The last caretaker

The last caretaker says:
No, it's not one of Grimm's tales
it's a country.
The Ones who defeated the Others
offer them a trip
to the Canary Islands.
Sewing little red riding hoods for export
getting used to the wolf.
(Hansel and Gretel still haven't
returned from abroad.)
The Others are now conductors
at the Metro stations.
They sell tickets and ask travellers
how much sun?   what's the time?
Days grow longer already. It isn't yet time.
Wolves starve. Little red riding hoods
export rejects
are sent back to the home market.
Apart from that elections are held
for conjurors and acrobats.
Herb books and crewcuts come back in fashion.
Yellowed old ladies
spin in front of shops
on merry-go-rounds.
Five in the morning approaches
but heavy and uncertain.
Only the insane beauty of the landscape
catches me up sometimes
and we die like everything else
that lives its moment.
Conversation time is over.
Behind the last caretaker of disaster
the gate closes.

(1985)

13

Instruction manual

I'm trying to get the country started.
I study the instruction manual carefully.
I turn the nation to the left.
I turn the nation to the right.
But the country doesn't work.
The nation's dead.
I try out revolutions.   Uprisings.   Different keys.
I lay ambushes following the directions exactly
but the country doesn't work.
The nation's dead.
Grass overgrows the battlefields.
Theories rust.
Red lights flash on.
I switch on the nation.
I switch off the nation.
I hug crime to my breast.
I give children
chocolate soldiers.
Marzipan rockets.
But the nation's dead.
Finally I submit a complaint.
The allied stretcher-bearers
Turquoise Angels
install spare parts.
But the nation's dead.
Somebody sells off the language
to casual buyers.
Someone else reels
thunderstruck
because nothing works but death
programme ninety-nine.

From the cemetery terminus
a tram pulls out
carrying riot victims.
The controllers
inspect tickets as usual.

(1990)

14

Trying

As we tried to talk to each other
it turned out
we had different tongues.
As we began to speak
a single language
we were robbed of speech.
As we came down from the hills
now we were united
by only the shadows of the dead.

(1985)

29 days

Every yet another biography
gives me a pain.
The Italian scientist Petrucci
grew life in a test-tube
for 29 days.
A poet I know jumped
from the third floor
– now his poems are much better.
The Italian scientist Petrucci
tricked the whole world.
The poet I know was born
again. In a test-tube.
And made a living writing for the rest of his life
for 29 whole days.
Quite a trick – said his nearest and dearest.

(1967)

Unprintable

Born in the laboratory
an orphan by preconception,
I declare
that my sister
born in the bedroom of the twentieth century
lost my mechanical doll
that for me replaced
an angel.

The Experiment
The Ultimately Successful Attempt
put on display in football stadiums
medicine's collective child
with the noose of tenderness round my neck,
I beg the honest finder
to return the doll
that can never be replaced by
an angel.

The doll's distinguishing features:
it speaks out two unprintable words
mummy   daddy.

(1974)

The first day of spring

When at four in the morning
I see my grandmother
flying over the city
with a shopping bag
her shoes worn out again
a cloak spread over her sleep –
I try to stop her
with Chinese whispers.
I draw the net curtains.
I wipe plankton from the stairs.
My grandmother stands in the queue.
Peers about her for bait.
No-one can resolve anything now.
To anyone's advantage.

The first day of spring
emigrates from the calendar.

(1985)

18

The citizen of a small country

The citizen of a small country
Thoughtlessly born on the edge of Europe
is called up to contemplate freedom.
As a reservist he'd never given it a thought.
He interrupts his whale's morning feed.
He leafs through dictionaries.
Several times before
he had passed through freedom with a transit visa.
Sometimes he stopped for lunch
and a glass of orange juice.
Sometimes it was
the underground stations.
The tunnels' black sleeves.
The cable cars over chasms.
Yet he always returned.
To his whale collection.
To the progressive dry cleaners
who had just been awarded
the order of the express.
To the great Agencies
denying the general meteorological situation.
To slips of the tongue
announcing great transformations.
To his private domain of freedom
where he walked
in a life-jacket
with a first-aid box on his shoulder.
These spaces greet him at night.
He is hunted by fear in a man's black glove.
At last the Northern Lights appear to him.

He is hanged
by his own hand
in victory square.
What has he chosen? – he asks himself.
The lesser absurdity
or a still bigger problem?

(1985)

Fear

Don't ask about the Carthaginians.
They died of fear.
Don't ask what to do about him.
Where to lead him.
To which wild goose chase.
Where to abandon him. Lose him.
When every time
he loops back like a boomerang.
I handed him long-distance tickets
and continents.
I killed him in dark alleys
and open spaces.
I helped him to some poison.
I appealed to God and the police.

Now he's playing an angel.
He hangs up his wings in the hall
and stares at me
with the eye
of a dead mackerel.

(1985)

Anxiety

I feel anxious. I'm worried about a woman
who has been dead for seven hours.
What happens to her next?
I'm worried about her child
seven hours older
who has burst a glass into tears.
I'm worried about our time
grown old beyond its years.
Millions of disasters slaughtered themselves
during the seven hours. Rivers drowned.
Torn clouds lay in the rain. Battles
fought centuries ago
returned where they belong. New battlefields
flew in eagerly.
Milliards of truths were proclaimed. Quadrillions
of decrees. Two suspects
were detained in the quarantine:
Adam and Eve.
(God looks at it all
sitting in the kitchen
and twirling spaghetti round his fork)

An eye-witness
to a universal loss of sight
I'm worried
about my world. But
in detonations of colour
carefree like a comic book
it revels in fanfares. The hot muscles
of continents explode. The icebergs burn.

But something else – poetry. A pinch of poetry
managed to break free.
What happens to her next?

(1972)

21

That night I was a murderer

That night I was a murderer.
I do not know the victim. It did not fight.
Perhaps it even waited for the fatal blow.
I gave it a present, a wreath with a pink bow.

I had no time to drag it from my steep sleep.
Again and again I fell running down to the graveyard.
The dead were surprised I didn't take a sledge
when all was white as spilt cream.

The unconscious lay along the bobsleigh track.
The dark solitude of our collective thoughts.
A shelter for hermits   outlaws   and lovers.
No-one could run us over
for a festival of redemption fell that day.

(1990)

Homunculus speaking

Look at that landscape
all aluminium space and light.
Sterile constructions of gardens.
Overgrown flower-beds of notions and truths.

In casinoes
men give birth to pale babies.
Fairy godmothers are running. Ward sisters.
Dogs howl.

Locked in test-tube tower blocks
magic children
are weeding their snacks.
The bird inherits no wings any more.
It's remotely controlled.

Never fall asleep
when spoken to by
the dwarf
Homunculus
choking to death
on some chemical elixir.

(1990)

Curriculum vitae

My life is like night
in the tractor factory.
Empty floors.
The walk-through rooms of Europe.
A foreigner in taxidermy air.

A hydrangea grows on the rented balcony.
A borrowed view of Yellowstone Falls.
Loneliness on discount in a used furniture store.

In the drawers of escritoires, in chests, wardrobes
an abandoned abacus. A china doll.

I rummage through other people's homelands.
I squander time
running away from myself.
I don't reach my hand out to the drowning.
I drown with them.

Calling for help
would be risky.
Calling on reason
superficial.

One day surely
I'll turn terrorist.
I'll hijack the country
that gave me language.

From that thought
nothing can save me
not even a lightning-rod.

(1990)

Questions at a poetry reading

Your favourite colour?
Luckiest day?
The poem that outran your imagination?
Don't you have any hope?
You frighten us.
Why the black sky
why time shot down?
The empty hand   a hat sailing the ocean?
Why a wedding dress
with a funeral wreath?
Hospital corridors
in place of forest tracks?
Why the past and not the future?
Do you have faith? Or don't you?
You frighten us.
We run away from you.

I try to stop them.
They fly straight into the flame.

(1982)

Lunar eclipse

The first sentence. A motionless lizard
in the quarries of a room.
Headache. Stuffed emptiness.
I can't hear a single idea.

I look through binoculars at grey paper fibres.
The blackmailer's already waiting at the door.
At that moment Hölderlin
has a tantrum. I lean

over a full stop. Mournful punctuation.
A black island with a bay's squeezed throat.
I watch a lunar eclipse.
I have to think about the rest.

(1991)

2

See It Everywhere

See it everywhere

1

I could have a child. But
what can I show it other than
– motorways
driving at excessive speed
– a waterfall
halted in its dive
– a peepshow
indifferent to it all?

How can I explain to it
– that only afternoons happen
to be happy
– that silence
is the most precise answer
– that history's winters
freeze heroes alive?
How can I explain to it
that we
twenty-four-year-olds
released on bail from the nursery
not yet graduated from the kindergarten
already belong in
the Old Folks' Home.
We lose balance
in empty space.

My child
could be born in uniform
with a line of fire on its palm, not a lifeline
with a helmet, not a silver spoon.
It could lose the freedom
it never possessed.

But also
it could find itself cherished
like orchids or *Gentiana Clusii*
or edelweiss floating its raft through the sky.

My child's not here. But
I hear its laughter and see it everywhere.
I see it sliding down a banister
of stairs which stepped down long ago.

2

My child hovers in the heavens.
My child comes into my mind.
My child is persecuted.
Constantly summonsed to the world.

My child hovers in the heavens
on crutches. No little legs. They haven't come in yet.
They've only got as far as Roanne
the little town in Burgundy.

My child comes into my mind.
It rises in front of me like the highest peak in the Alps
I'll never reach. It holds small hands out from the snow.
Stares with an eye's frozen cornea.

My child is persecuted.
Constantly summonsed to the world by warrants.
By bloodhounds. By the Department of Statistics.
By gloves bought in the sale.
Already on earth awaiting my child are
my child's years.

And the heavens sag
under a glut of berries.

(1972)

29

We look at the photos

Who is your grandad and why does that matter?
What's the ancestry of Friday and Saturday?
How about the pigeon cooing in your ear?
Why do your dreams reach so far ahead?
Much too far for our times.

We look at the photos of Hitler in nappies.
We look at the photos of other babies
who shook the world.

(1972)

My sister

My sister doesn't know, not yet
that they sentenced the world to an atlas.
And the atlas is a huge and ever-hungry plate.
A country-pattern knitting magazine. Some styles out of date.
That everything becomes clear after you leave the movies.
That ideas hang better on dummies.
That death's never an example.
That death is for nature.
That before watching the skies
you must take them to the censor.
That the library of space contains the greatest wisdom.
That love is love. And love is a garden.
That in that garden you must avoid autumn.
That in that garden no-one avoids autumn.
That nothing stops the cell's division.
That life has its ending the second it begins.
That Isolde is old. Suffers from rheumatism.
That history is some kind of giant bin.
For frightening children and to waste dates in.
That when for a while night draws shadows on our eyes
birds wake inside us.   'The Earth! The Earth!'   they cry.
And then we discover a new continent: Man
who brushes our eyelids with his warm hand . . .

But my sister does already know
that A is for apple

(1970)

Children's home

Thirty pairs of felt slippers
with tulip blossom appliquéd on the toe.
Thirty little smocks blotted with blackcurrant
juice. Thirty motionless cats
embroidered with a chain stitch.
Thirty pairs of little hands reaching up
but only for porridge spoons.
Thirty pairs of eyes opening wide in sleep
to catch a glimpse of parents on the candy hills.

If my mummy wanted to
she could be queen.
But she had to die
because daddy turned into a wolf.

My mummy was thin
so she couldn't love me.
But soon as she gets un-thin
she'll buy me forever.

My mummy is beautiful. My daddy is strong.
My mummy is rich. She could buy
North America and gold. And daddy
can shoot a real gun.

Thirty pairs of little legs
stand at the disused railway points
awaiting the approach
of a home.

(1972)

Children

Children get together for nostalgia nights.
Children get together at executive sessions.
Children have experience.
Some do not know about swans.

Children have identity cards. Birth certificates.
Case histories. Death certificates.
Children choose the leader who
makes a speech on the rocking horse.

Children kidnap ministers and aeroplanes.
Children emigrate to the ends of the earth.
Children inform on their parents.
Children fight for the rights of dolls.
Children sit in astrakhan furs.
Pink cakes float in the air.
Children remember the Imperium Romanum
and sadly nod their little heads.

In the vast nursery of nations
children play ball and
spit cherry stones at one another.
They switch on an artificial sun
that rises like a mitigating circumstance.
Then children put their toys away
and earnestly start to work
on new children.

(1972)

Dawn

A twelve-year-old girl dies of leukemia.
Tubs of pomegranates stand in the hospital corridor.
It's New Year's Eve and canned flowers are blossoming.
The girl's brother Zenobius has come
tonight he has proposed to his beloved
and the moment he says goodbye to his sister they will go
to a ball in a mountain hut in Biała Polana.
Meanwhile inside the twelve-year-old girl
a massively sick town grows up with a square and a fountain
anaemic as light. With a petrol station.
With a pub, 'Vain Hope'. A riven acacia tree
struck by lightning. Three churches.
A vagrant who drifts forever in dreams.
A school that graduated to form 7A.
The twelve-year-old girl asks her brother
to fetch the navy-blue notebook from home.
She'll do her biology. She has to catch up.
Beyond the window night staggers like a brewery.
Zenobius says goodbye. Reaches out to his sister.
A bottle of vodka in his pocket gets in his way.
Zenobius goes into the mountains. His sister the opposite way.
And dawn sails between them down the level river bed.

(1972)

34

Nothing's certain

You might turn into a madman.
You might exchange the currency of madness for genius.

Nothing's certain.

Out of ten witnesses
present in court
the eleventh will testify
you're guilty.

They might bring you a nation in a briefcase.
You might dote on it from fear
or love.

You might grow vegetables
that poison you.

Your weapon collection
might shoot you dead.

You might be lucky tomorrow
even though it's Tuesday.

Nothing's certain.

Even the cancer in my tissue
isn't certain of tomorrow.

(1974)

No title

Don't wait for me. Shut down the trees.
They'll understand. They were made that way.
Say nothing to the leaves. They needn't be told.
Let them turn their faces to the world's fifth side.
Shut the doors tight. That's enough for them.
But not with a key. Just pretend.
You can tell the wind. It will shake its arms
and blow through the night. A good alibi.
And do tell the windows that watch our house
with their eyes forever open wide awake.
That's all. Don't tell anybody else.
Push off the unrelenting cloudy clouds.
Don't wait for me and leave your voice closed.
The night is too steep. Stay away from it.
The night is too steep, don't wait for me.
I won't come today. Now I have to die.

(1967)

Grudgingly

And if I really died – nothing would happen.
The family would cluster with black banners.
They might even manage to cry for a moment.
The sun would move as usual. And waggling their legs children
would sit high up on the clouds.
No-one would stop the doorbells   the visits   the telephones
elections of a new Napoleon   a new Chagall
a new hat for summer. And the old
Bible would still be old.

You might sit down for a moment
open your hands wide
and stare   stare   stare.
Only for a moment. No more.

Therefore
I die grudgingly.

(1967)

Bird

The child was born abnormal.
A volcano cried out from its mouth
and froze in the air.
Fire glared from its eyes
and set the house ablaze.
You can only look at the child when it's asleep.
Then it looks like an angel
that fell on its head.
But the child knows something
and tries to warn us of something.
To do so
it joined a consonant course.

After fifty years
the child decided to turn into a bird.
Now it flies around the neighbourhood.
You can recognize it late in the evening
when it shoots off suddenly and cries
'Humans!'
and all the other birds
scatter screaming.

(1972)

The recipe

Suicide
should be committed after breakfast.
For breakfast you should have a glass of
milk.
Milk contains plenty of vitamin A.
Vitamin A protects you from disorders of
the eye.
The eye is for seeing.
And what you should see is
the world.

Suicide
should be committed so quietly.
As quietly
as though a fly walked across
a violin string
releasing a downy sound or perhaps
just sighing.

And the crumbs from your bread
should be scattered for the birds.
So they might go on living.
So they might go on
living.

(1970)

From a letter II

Say, how can you commit suicide in this place, love
when you're a corpse anyway?
'Cause how can you live in
this slimy time of ours?
You can't pull your hand out
to squeeze the trigger of a gun
nor drown in it.
And when you look at it all, love
it's black   black   black
like widows on strike.
Our Annie got married.
She's having a baby.
We're all happy.

(1974)

* * *

I wasn't saved by the flood
though I already lay on the bottom.

I wasn't saved by the flames
though I burned for years.

I wasn't saved by disasters
though trains and cars ran over me.

I wasn't saved by the planes
that exploded with me in mid-air.

Great city walls
collapsed on me.

I wasn't saved by poisonous mushrooms
or the sharp shots of firing squads.

I wasn't saved by the end of the world
since it had no time for me.

I wasn't saved at all.

I'M ALIVE.

(1978)

* * *

So what if he's mediocre?
At least he's happy.
What? He's like a rattle?
So he can entertain babies.
I'm sure he's got lots more readers
than he has.
He likes hearing his own poems.
They tickle his ears.
They go to bed with him
like wedding nights.
And as soon as he rubs sleep from his eyes
his calling calls him:
hop   hop
hop   hop

Only God
to whom he compares his talent
said calmly:
oh no – no chance.

(1978)

* * *

I didn't become a great statesman.
I didn't discover a continent.

I didn't write a masterpiece
that would shake the world.

I couldn't even run to a great murder.

I didn't set anyone's house on fire
(no – a house was burnt in me)

I never set anyone an example.
Neither bad. Nor good.
Incapable of love and of hate.

With a lack of character
pinned on my lapel.

Sentenced for mediocrity
I die indifferently.

The fly
that for hours
has looked at me blankly
must be my alter ego.

(1978)

Class 1

Why, yet again, is Robespierre late for school
coming after the bell, torturing silence?
Leaving his head behind, playing the fool?
He looks a mess. D minus for your life.

Why doesn't Homer know the structure of the atom
shutting his eyes to whatever's on the board?
These tricks won't do him a bit of good at home:
his anxious parents should be told the truth.

Who told Mozart to look out of the window?
And why did Einstein just push him aside
and stare at the empty space, giggling wildly
believing his theory, not believing in sin?

Why does Mann – Thomas! – pretend this is all his own
work? Tomorrow I want to see your mum here please!
Why's Plato eating his lunch in the classroom?
Laura, leave Petrarch in peace!

I can't go on teaching a class like this
one moment longer.
Today several islands fell off
the globe on my desk.
Where's the history monitor?

– Herodotus? He just bunked off.

(1970)

Special bulletin

Children playing hopscotch
stay unaware of
the future.
That sweet schizophrenia of theirs:
the little whipped-cream snowmen
a meadow of crickets
the instinct of a blue cornflower
– alternating
with the reason
of parents gamblers
shysters murderers
forgers spies thieves.
That sweet schizophrenia of theirs
with pink cheeks.
An earthly event
with all the consequences.
Children's don't yet know
that Citoyen Guillotin invented the machine
that cut his head off.
They're careless. Never listen to their elders.
They ask: why?
and without waiting for the answer
they stick fingers in their ears
put chocolate dips in their mouths
and rush far away.
To their place.

(1972)

45

Why are you so glad you survived?

Why are you so glad you survived?
You dance round the burnt house.
Who are you glad for?
The sole survivor.
Not even a mouse escaped. Nor a bat.
Nor a pipit nor a death's-head moth.
Nor grass. Nor a stone.
How do you cry when the voice didn't survive?
Who do you cry to when the ear didn't survive?
What will you do with your death that survived?
Your heart beats. Your arms wave.
Does that mean goodbye or hello?
You can't even hurl yourself off anything.
(There are no mountains)
Or drown.
(There are no oceans)
Or poison yourself.
(Oleander's vanished)

The weasles
you wear
can bite you to death
if you're lucky.

(1982)

Place

'This is no place for painting'
said Degas and he crept away from heaven
back to Montmartre.

The hill gathered its colours together
stretched in its frame of alleys
and rose to meet him.

But only the quiet wisps of clouds were circling.
The dancers had flown. The butterflies were gone.
Paint spilt into rivers.

'This is no place for painting'
said Degas and he opened the Larousse
at the entry *Panta rhei*.

(1970)

Such times

I walk across the playground. And all of a sudden
a six-year-old boy rushes to me
with wild strawberry cheeks.
In his hand he clutches a pop gun.
'Bang! Bang!' – he shoots at me.
Then he sticks his weapon in his pocket.
'Gotcha!' – he says and runs off.

I notify the family. Friends.
I phone the police and report my death.
They spread their helpless hands.
'Such times' – they say.

(1972)

Perhaps it will be better

Perhaps it will be better when I return
to this house.
I'll take the lift to the seventh floor. I'll ring
the bell of this flat.
'They moved out a long time ago.'
'Yes,' I'll say, 'but they forgot to take
the bedclothes that reconciled them. The room
from which there was always a way out.
The whisper of hands that touch. They forgot about
the violin note left in the air. About a night
long as a hallway. About a night stopped
in a tunnel. They forgot about the child
who seventeen years ago
left for school
form 1C to get there for eight.
And about hope wrapped in a newspaper
that should be lying in the left-hand corner of the wardrobe.
And about the raincoats.
So I'm sure you'll understand,
the rain.
More and more often that rain . . .'

(1972)

49

From a journey

We were on the same plane.
The same wing blinded our eyes.
We were eating a Chinese salad with olives.

You sat there in your usual shirt.
You smoked the same Winstons.
Your eyes studied the lakes of clouds.
The furrow in your right cheek.
The twist of your mouth.
It was your hand holding the newspaper.
Your smile smiled at the stewardess.

And when I called your name
you replied: sorry, you've taken me for someone else –
you said it with the voice I knew well.

And though seven years had passed
since your funeral
you hadn't changed at all.
Perhaps a bit too much death on you.
An empty watch on your wrist
and beyond the aeroplane window
pink night.

You give me a stranger's business card.
You offer your chill hand.
Your dead eyelid
reflects in the window.

They turn the lights on.
please fasten your seatbelts
The earth approaches.
Wreaths of the welcoming crowd.

(1982)

Two letters

You set out for San Francisco
and I'm dying.

Western Lines went on strike.
For the moment I'm lying in my room reading the papers.
I had a letter from Zet.

I'm a thousand miles from home.
In the world's best hospital.
The doctors shake their heads
in tender helplessness.

Zet writes that the world is coming to an end.
Send me some new poems.
I've grown fond of Maxwell House here.

You set out for San Francisco.
A radium cloud is sailing over me.
We won't finish this conversation I think.

Our letters crossed
somewhere in the middle of Europe.
Space mocked us.

On your grave I straighten
crushed ivy.
I button
a leaf's creased collar.

(1982)

Learn death

Learn death. By heart.
According to the spelling rules for
dead words.

Spell it in one word
like commonwealth or snapdragon.

Don't split it
amongst the dead.

You are gods' darling
Learn death early.

Love of your country
can be lethal too.

Learn death
in love.

Learn death not simply
to kill time.

Time can be suicidal
and hangs for hours from the trees.

Test yourself.
Test yourself alive.

(1978)

Goodbye, everyone

Goodbye, everyone.
I'm leasing the world
fully furnished.
Wardrobes of mountains and hills.
The carpet plains.
Volcano containers.
Cased continents and peninsulas.
Boxed air.
Bonnets of lakes
with bullrush feathers.
Desert hour-glasses.
Oceans in a beer can.
Northern Lights on the table.
Cartographic nets entwining
humans   animals   plants.
Shawls of ivy.
Cemeteries caked with rust.
A cobweb of time   a quartz cuckoo.

In the hospice
I visit my country.
On a newspaper-covered meadow
A smashed bottle.
In the window, a will-of-the-wisp.

Goodbye, everyone.
Behind the door
a granite whale
awaits me.

(1990)

Hands

for Dr. Maria Leńczyk

1

The corridor can lead you to the white Arctic.
And you may never return. Like Willem Barents.
The frost here is sharp as a lancet. And sometimes
the lancet is colder than the Arctic Circle.

A white trolley stands in the corridor.
Willem Barents' frozen ship.
Every object is here for a reason.
Even the four fire-extinguishers, like withered roses.

2

A bird of ether settled by my head.
I couldn't even plant tomatoes in my dream.
It wasn't an ordinary dream. There was such silence,
as if suddenly all the servants had deserted the house.

And then the silence softens. Then – the sea, the tide.
The operating theatre's pierced by a spark of illumination,
a green aurora seen from far away.
Close-up: it focuses onto two wise hands.

And on those two hands I swear.

(1970)

3
They

They

They're so in love that from that hate
they snatch their panther moments from the air
and secretly feeding them to savage one another
they fake shivers to attract the butterflies.

She says to him: I believe in you
like a ship on the open sea. And running in the meadow
she feels as safe as *plusquamperfectum*
the safest of tenses.
He – sees through her eyes which magnify
the bad and good sides of this world
equidistant from their slender legs.

They're so in love that from that hate
they kiss the prints on their fingers
and pack their cases. They lock
memory in cages. And throw the keys down
a raindrop. You can hear them hit the bottom.
And from that hate
they're so in love that at tea-time
they hand each other bunches of thyme
as if quite unexpectedly
they'd been invited by King Popiel, who in mad silence
served them bowls filled with the mice
who had devoured him.

Punctually late.   He and she.   They know
they don't live in the age of Sebastian Bach.
The fish's convex eye must be envious of
the way they look at all things with a wink.

(1970)

56

No way out

This is the hotel. This is the room.
The bed in which they slept.
Pink magnolias still hang in the wardrobe.
They infected almost the whole town with love.
People fell into each others' arms.
Little girls hung round the necks of men
like costume jewellery.
At the bureaux de change
they exchanged kisses.
People stopped dying.
Now the hearse carried newly-weds.
Bureaucrats read lyrics by Ronsard.
Censors crossed out the horizon.
They corrected the view from the window.
Watteau's *Fêtes Galantes*
was hung up in the middle of the square.
The loudspeakers broadcast
Dichterliebe
Schumann's songs.
Animals were fitted with wings
shaped like hearts.
The terror of love gripped the town.
Those who resisted were thrown down a chasm.
Is it possible not to want to love?
Someone tried to speak but made no sense.
Someone else had crime on the tip of his tongue.
Countless hordes of rats were quitting the town
without looking back at the fireworks.
People just danced at the compulsory ball.
And they alone already knew
that one step forward is simply death
and one step back merely murder.

(1990)

A free translation from Shakespeare

Your eyes still gaze in mine as when
– morning, year one, eleventh century –
caught in my billowing gown your knee
could not find its way out again.

Love never changes through the ages.
Stone was and still is made of stone.
The river was and still remains a river.
Eternal love will still be love forever.

And you still think the same of me
as the prince did, with whom I often
swung from the trees with agile grace
when I became his fair lady.

Love never changes through the ages.
Time wore its hooves out on my life.
You say goodbye to me as you said goodbye.
You say good-day to me as you said good-day.

Here once again through time's perversity.
Consigned to the protection of its hands.
Tick tock. Contemporary. Also middle-aged.
Tick tock. Sad. Happy. Argumentative.

Tick tock. Lights slowly going out.
Tick tock. In everlasting love
sleeps a contemporary prince. He's past.
Contemporary-past. He slips away.
Into the night. No fret no fuss.
As though his hand still clutched his lines,
good enough for Polonius.

(1967)

Last words

Perhaps it's better
it was too late
to share
those last words.

Last words
could fail us.

Too vividly
touch on things.

Heedless
they could knock against
the future tense.

Prematurely bury
something in us.

They might have
nothing to say.

They could talk
beyond all measure.

Tell us
far too everything.

Like an active volcano
under a tweed sky.

Perhaps it's better
we had no time
to share
those last words.

Locked inside the last words
a wood grouse.

(1978)

Confessions of a courtesan

'Most often they're afraid of the light' she says
snapping on her black garter. 'Of the Nation'
she opens her cigarette case. 'Accomplices'
she rests her leg on the bedstead.
'They're suspicious, look behind the curtains.
They invite me to parachute jumps
bulletproof cocktails in snug bars.
They call on me in emergencies.
I've got lots of souvenirs. Snapshots.
Medals. Newspapers.
The one on the left died. This one they shot.
Officially I run a
bridal hire boutique.
These gowns lived through many revolutions.
They witnessed *coups* of love.
In some you can still hear
The flutter of hearts. Flouncy white cages.'
She touches up the rouge on her cheek,
'They lose their glamour with the years
and fall off the shoulder.' She lights a cigarette,
'And one general
just to amuse me
ate all his insignia
and stayed till daybreak.
We like clients like that.
In these listless times
when the black swan in your eye
means ill fortune.'

(1985)

Confession of a man whose woman leaves like summer and returns like summer

You leave me
like summer.
And you return to me
like summer.
Unexpectedly you drive into the square   (Open Rally 1990
102 hp)
You for the last time. Me for the last time.
The last of my patience
but
not the last.
It's grown so much it'll last us
all our love.

Hope it won't.   Hope it will.

And you don't even switch off the lights.
You appear weightless like a car's shell.
There's more and more of you and less.
More or less you.
You appear unexpectedly like a disaster.
And as we both perish in the crash
there isn't a single soul
prepared to run us over clean through
(our love)
so you could no longer
leave me
like summer.
And return to me
like summer.

(1970)

61

Confessions of a rationalist

I don't go to church.
I meet the Lord God at the tailors'.
They're making us up the same grave.

(1990)

Confessions of an émigré

to Wacław Iwaniuk

They stole my motherland. From my satchel.
From her borders. They snatched her as
she went into the street.
Lucky night for the poachers.
They piled up such a haul.
First they sat her at the table.
Plied her with vodka. Motherland was struggling
but losing strength. Then they bought her
a red frock. A hat
with peacock feathers. They waved her
from the balcony during military parades.
Motherland's in a coma.
Perhaps she'll still be saved by the camomile
of the commonwealth rising.
But the dead spread their helpless arms.
The ambulance doesn't arrive.
There'll be no miracle.
To be continued
with just another lament –
says
a despairing émigré.

(1985)

A man who isn't all there
tries to pity the world

A man who isn't all there tries to pity the world. And he begs
next to the magnanimously Gothic church.
It's well past twelve
and one should consider the consequences.

– For the deaf and dumb dog
who never wanted to be born a dog.
– For the child I don't have
but who's hungry.
– For the woman who had her breast cut off.
The woman I don't love.
– For the soldier who's homeless
but owns his grave.
– For all those who evade death
which never fails you.
– For the whole world whose brakes failed
so it speeds up   and up
and up.
– For the labours of time.

(1970)

A moment

That fluffy squirrel
suddenly has something human to tell me.

That butterfly has settled next to me
not by mere chance.

A bird looks at me
with an eye I know.

The thrush's cry warns me
against killing time.

How do I know that silence
dropping from the owl's mouth?

The grimace of a tired lioness
from behind too-human bars.

The dog's freedom
of whole nations
how trustingly it looks into my eyes.

That wolf's howl. The moth's suicide.
A friend must be calling for my help.

That moment
clutches me suddenly
and pounds my heart
against cool air.

(1978)

65

Voice

I am too old   too late
to decide what to do.

I wish I hadn't failed to promise
anyone anything ever.

Two women whom I loved
took their lives.

One of them
I often meet in the library.

All I can do now is take the VOICE
for long walks.

It runs far ahead of me
when I unmuzzle it outside town.

That VOICE
often calls me aside.

Or drags me to it
with its wretched whine.

As a sign perhaps
that in life I missed
something crucial — —

(1978)

Funeral

First snow this year.
China dog out of breath.
Stone angel.
A land covered in a sheet.
A woman receding down a cemetery lane
unfurls black sails.
Not one star fell down from the heavens
before my eyes
the priest admits.
But we still hope.
In a moment
the coffin
the submarine
will sink
in earth.

(1990)

The Black Monastery of Bats

I was time's accomplice
but I declare myself bankrupt.
I took no account of the flitting years.
I stopped too long at
the Marine Bed Museum
in San Francisco
the beauty and ugliness salon
searching for the distinction
between fate and chance.
I waited too long
for a train to Murnau.
I was stopped by the seizures
of my dear departed
preceding earthquakes
and volcanic eruptions.
A fountain of green olives
during supper at the Cannettis.
Bells at the door
behind which no-one waited.
I stood too long in front of Vermeer's painting
the *Woman Reading a Letter*
never turned to me.
I tried to steal the world's beauty.
I rolled up landscapes like carpets
and carried hours away to the north.
I waited in vain for a taxi
driving off to the Last Moment.

Ahead of me a steep hill.
Narrow path. The pointing hands
of wild tulips.
The Black Monastery of Bats.

(1990)

60 minutes of solitude

On the beach. In hot bedclothes of sand.
By the plummeting roar of the wave.
At the horizon   Dramatic Irony
a ten-year-old girl
takes wing on a surfboard.
The species' alien voice
crawls out from the wreck
of my imagination.
A criminal's sweating hands
leaf through the pages
of a music manuscript.
A motionless flock of flamingoes.
A chair stands in the desert.

I breathe the new
incomprehensible
dialect of the air.

(1990)

Poet?   Criminal?   Madman?

He conceives his world from start to finish.
A pale province of paper where he grows pink zinnias.
He dreads imagination
the desert blasting sand in his eyes and mouth.
When he imagined a flood
water drowned the town.
He loved a poet and arms dealer.
At night he read his verses.
Illuminations, A Season in Hell
He dies with him.
Yet not for long.
Reality steams all around.
Coffins grow in meadows.
Instead of a forest,   a forest's powdered wig.
Instead of air,   orchids of smoke.
Lover of nature
he nurses a river in the sink.
He dodges the lighthouse
that beams omens at him.
He dies a second time
from a freedom attack.
Then again
seeks refuge in language
which like all living species
is ripe for cruelty and treason.
He's woken by the scream of the past.

No-one knows anything about him.
It's said that passing through the valley of childhood
he bit a viper.

(1990)

René's come home

Dead poets come home
in the *cortèges* of clairvoyant biographers
metamorphic boys
patrolling the Thesaurus.
Rose bouquets
run wild in their hands
into vast plantations.
They stay in *pensions*
framed with school uniforms.
René's come home   calls Greta
from the Alps in Wales. We must do a cherry dessert.
Someone's already seen him on the Matterhorn.
Poor pale Mr. Rilke
with a migraine iceberg on his brow
and a white bat bow-tie.
He already knows how to be dead
and he treats the life of a small town
as an insoluble event.

(1991)

71

Time's recipients

The taxed recipients of time.
Rebels hide in philosophy's extinct volcanoes.
They run down the fireproof staircase
to the white paper plains.
Dignified gentlemen drag
caterwauling heroes:
the murderers of young girls. Exhibitionists.
Nymphomaniacs. Discarded lovers.
Novels written
under a psychic pseudonym.
Young Torless.   Joseph K.   Leopold Bloom.
We are all alike
and we look like shares falling
or a lethal telegram.

(1991)

Forgive me that . . .

I don't answer your letters   phonecalls.
I discard friendships.

Forgive me that . . .

I grow more and more tied to myself.
I draw back into the depths.

The nation doesn't amaze me.
The crowd doesn't amaze me.

Victories and defeats melt into one.
Gains and losses melt into one.

On the heath I admire a butterfly.
At night I feed bats.

From the mountain peak
I watch
the setting oyster of the sun.

Forgive me that . . .

(1985)

To Marianna Büttrich

I've already tried for a year
to write you a letter.
But
the locust of my thoughts
is untranslatable.

Untranslatable janitors
guard my words and grammar.

Untranslatable my hours
into your hours.

An elderflower outside the window.
Unbuttoned gates. The yellowed butt-ends of the day.

A dead eye in the spyhole
first thing in the morning.

Untranslatable Rilke.

Die Blätter fallen, fallen . . .
Wir alle fallen . . .

I have so much to tell you
but
a tunnel looms
towards my delayed train.

The lingering whistle.

I'm tired Marianna,
I'm off for a rest
in the Bermuda Triangle.

(1985)

4
A Substitute Life

We choose freedom

We choose freedom.
We set off from the coast.
The foreign language of the heavy oars.
Speech constrains us.
In the little town Neumarkt
at eight in the morning
the proprietors of freedom
lay out herrings.
Lanterns. Lights. Cheerful houses.
A smiling cyclist.
We buy ink. Breathe in the lavender air.
Pull a suitcase on a leash.
Lonely mountaineers
on a conquered peak.

(1990)

A substitute life

I've started to think about a substitute life.
I'm perched on the roof of the year that's ending.
I needn't save insurance any more
for the ship.
I sail away rejecting the laws of geometry.
Comic writers take their cases
to the left-joke office.
Next to me a Flemish anatomist.
Fedon – the bawdy-house doorman.
We discuss Giotto's frescoes.
We watch an upholsterer
cover a piece of earth
with fresh grass. He spreads the fabric
over the multiplying plains.
We drip forty-five milligrams of incidents
into a lake's eye.
Rambling tourists
dead for several miles
we darn our substitute life.

(1991)

* * *

Why don't you try and do something human?
Don't be posthumous.

Why don't you show some spark of interest?
Don't abuse death.

Why don't you finally
beat
the grave?

Don't decorate yourself
with the cross.

Even in the sealed hour-glass coffin
a desert swirls.

(1982)

New York the hijacked city

Stewardesses of the clouds above the Atlantic.
O stewardesses of the clouds.

We land at La Guardia
together with advertisements for Ozark Air Lines
Dutch Heineken beer   and the fountain of eternity pen
Parker 75 *(The Parker Company)*
with which I write a letter to my Departed Friend:

(Don't trust death,
that you've died forever.

I'm desperately tired
don't rob me of illusions.

In the endless space
there is a House for the Dead)

I won't write a poem about New York.
Thousands of poems have been written about New York.
A polyglot crowd of words
demonstrating on Fifth Avenue.

With poetry banners
a photocopied crowd
pasted up on walls
in the aquarium of air.

With a minute bacterium
spirillum minus
with fingers caught in the door
of events.

I won't write a poem about New York.
Spread out in verse,   Manhattan
moves off slowly like a freight train
infected with the plague of time.

I can see my reflection in the black-ringed eyes
of that forever insomniac city.
On white paper sheets
I record sleep.

Wind blowing from the Atlantic
drifts my words away
into the shallows of meaning.

A spiky cactus dawn rises
in Times Square.

Such a rustle of dictionaries.
Murmuring mouths.
For one hour of silence.

'So much life. So much life.
For one moment of death'   a tourist says.

'New York is very tiring'
'yes, it is'   replies another.

The travel agent armed them
with a pocket phrasebook
which helps them
swallow the city.

With taste and smell guidebooks.
With a transparent sky of brochures.

In the Museum of Modern Art
my blood scan is hanging.

The tourists open catalogues
and enter them
subdivided into groups
voices and nations.

From the fifty-ninth floor
of the Pan Am Building
I observe
the hopeless escape of light
from the General Motors electric sign.

Oceans of hope flying away.

In the bar of the Piccadilly Hotel
on 227 W 45th Street
I sit
between epochs
like a bookmark.

I hang up history in the cloakroom.
There
events swing
unclaimed for years.

Crossed out of a disaster
dug out from the white avalanche
of hospital corridors
I escape the dead.

But even here they stare at me
from beyond frozen windows
from beyond the dead side
and shriek: treason treason.

How come you're here?
How come we're there?

We have to sleep on the dead side
and you on the living. Against us.

And the plaster that peels off the wall
it's only snow it's only snow.

And I can find no words for them.
What could I leave them as a gift –
Perhaps geraniums carved in stone.

And the plaster that peels off the wall
it's only snow it's only snow.

You say to me:
certainty's deserting us already
we're entering beautiful times.

At Pennsylvania Station
I send a letter to my Departed Friend:

(Why don't you try and do something human?
Don't be posthumous.)

I won't write a poem about New York.
I won't describe the city
that walks through me
like fog through Triboro Bridge.

I won't describe the rock climbers
reaching the peak of the Empire State Building
falling into populated loneliness
smashing themselves
against every instant of air.

New York hangs on me
like an oversized coat.

'You shouldn't carry this town on your shoulders'
a waiter says to me.

I leave him a tip
for thought service.

In the Piccadilly Hotel
in room No 207

I pack New York into my cases.

With the city's excess baggage
at the airport I wave my friends goodbye.
We rise
crossing the boundaries.

Down there still:
the last subway train
with no station
falls onto an empty plain.

Down there still:
blue and grey paper air
meticulously wraps
the abandoned hotel
at the torn-off collar of the street.

Down there still:
the receding hydrangeas of
the abyss.

Stewardesses of the clouds above the Atlantic.

The city's yellowing scarf
emerges from my suitcase.

(1982)

Tourist group

They've booked me the language and the country.
It could be worse though it's not the best.
On the map it's just a restaurant table.
Fingerprint table cloth.
Four governesses were always at my side.
The first kept adjusting my thoughts and collars.
The second fell down the stairs leading to Monte Cavallo.
The uneven number of steps
was supposed to bring good luck.
From the third I contracted a sneer.
At bed-time the fourth   a police colonel
read me letters from informers.
It all seemed normal.
A tourist group trying to find their way.
The sun didn't hesitate for an instant.

(1990)

84

The open border

Along the open border
nets spread out.
The yellowed bulb of the sun.
Hunters have set their snares.
You are the forbidden pamphlet.
Your hat smuggles your head.
Your head smuggles thoughts.
My dear departed
open their suitcases.
Black suit.
White shirt.
Underwear laid bare.
The audience rises.
Customs officers pluck out of sleeves
bright hankies balloons bugles.
The dogs bark.
The wall falls.

(1990)

For instance in Kurfürstendamm

For instance in Kurfürstendamm.
As Frau Friedrich comes out
from the Wertheim department store.
A group of young people. Coloured balloons.
Inflatable rockets.
Inflatable coffins the colour of rainbows.
Acrobats on the high voltage wires.
Somebody spreads wings.
A white dwarf in silver fox furs
with a small red star on his hat.
The street stands still.
Vendors of ice-cream materialise.
Of hot-dogs.   Coca-Cola.
See-through flags.   Leaflets.   Ribbons.
Tinned doves of peace.
The breeders rub their hands.
More and more white doves.
Cyclones of white doves.
Typhoons of white doves.
A hurricane of applause.
Thousands killed and wounded.
Deserted towns. Shattered houses.
The torn tapestry sky.

Frau Friedrich
nods her head sadly.
She straddles a swing
and flies off to Güntzelstrasse.

(1990)

Supervision

Freedom chose this landscape
so we must keep it under supervision.
We sprinkle perfume on the forests.
We're taking charge of the hotel
where you'll both be staying.
Four streets adjoining. A bus stop.
A viaduct over the ravine's black wing.
We inspected your suitcases
as a precaution against Pharaoh's ants.
But you brought nothing with you.
Only a snowy owl and a polar chill.
We recommend our local speciality
 'truite à la bleu'
 cooked in white wine with vegetables.
'La petite danseuse' as they say in France.
Evening strolls along the heatproof beach.
A preselected vista of weddingcake yachts.
We supervise everything
as you can see.

We've even summoned a diviner
to our church
to ensure God
isn't standing
on a water table.
Well
even faith needs watchmen.

(1990)

A young German at a poetry reading

My name is Albrecht Dürer
but I'm not a painter.
I never wrote a book on castle fortification
nor on human proportions.
13 male types 13 female types.
I live in a small town Marburg in Augustinergasse.
Now Gottfried Benn's ghost sells sausages here.
I belong to the Greens. I'm thirty-five years old.
I've been to Auschwitz.
I used a can opener
to open the past.
I don't want to amortize history
although I'm a lawyer.
I don't want to be guilty forever
just because I'm German.
Sometimes I dream about scrapyards.
About handrails over an abyss.
I saw communism at close quarters.
Small red stars in the mouldy sky.
In the trees instead of leaves
grey coats swung.
I tamed the doves of peace.

Tell me,   do you think mankind's insane?
Insane,   incomprehensible,   aren't they the same?

(1990)

The misanthrope's vacation

He chooses volcanic islands.
Plains with wide open windows
from which he watches
if anyone comes.

He avoids traps.
The thought of falling
into someone's sentence
drowns him in silence.

He often dies at night
but there's always a live ending.

He scornfully observes
a ship-town passing.
Three hotels.   Restaurants.   Bars.
Stadiums.   Discotheques.   A Church.

He hears the human chassis
grinding.

He brings an avalanche of Haydn
down on himself
and at its foot
wrapped in a woollen blanket
sobs with emotion.

(1990)

The short-stay parking zone

From.   To.   The misleading life-line
intersects at the prohibited point
with busy Bismarkstrasse.

With Siberian tundra,
Christmas Eve in a winter coat
buttoned by death.

With shrinking towns. Tiny houses
like sunflower seeds.

With the cradle of a valley
swallowed by earth.
With a derailed childhood
in a toy museum.

Those
who've made it
die on the golf course.

For those
whose years proliferate
others prepare doctrines and plagues.

History nett. History gross.

The world exchanges names. Addresses.
Funeral halls of diaries.

The duty-free   short-stay
parking zone.

(1990)

Pyrron 1990

The man walking downstairs
suspending all judgement
the Sophists' rival
talking to himself
the victim of greedy metaphors
which swallowed the fat iambics
and left him nothing but doubts
likes archival excursions.
He spends his vacation in Antiquarium
an old multipaged resort.
He likes young coin collectors.
Cheque forgers.
Perhaps he's just a genius
condemned to a common journey
on the underground.
Asked by a neighbour in the lift
about life after death
he replies: it's just the emergency exit.

(1991)

The hitch-hiker

O friend, you too will die. But why do you complain?
Alas, Patroclus also died, a man better than you.

Homer

Stop that hearse. Well, it will stop anyway.
Say a few words in the official state language.
You can admire the natural resources of the country
you go to. The metric system.
Diamonds. Sugar. Tobacco products.
Don't try to prove that truth's an odd number.
Don't count on an answer.
The name of the country you're entering
is Cataract.

(1991)

Boat house

Young poets
who go out for a walk
at three in the morning
sing in a choir of angels.
They weave plaits
from waterfalls.
The closest relatives of Dylan Thomas
light candles on the beach.
They cast their nets over
the inflowing shoal of words
a flood without borders.

(1991)

A report for Alan Brooke Turner

England the Insular Lady
tight Victorian collar
buttoned to her neck.
Instead of rouge the rusty dust of ages.
Charles Dickens' ghost disappears round the corner.
Inside a pearl Rolls-Royce coffin
the lid rises. In the Bonnington Hotel
I drink chocolate and die
from excess of life
and from the left-sided traffic   *keep left.*
Taxis in black tuxedos
take me to the sixth floor.
A squadron of top hats
is flying above me now.
Valerie Connor hands me schedules
tickets   cash.   I roll up
the smiling Queen.
Next day it's already Wales.
Barbara and I stay in a village.
Hours that were to prolong our lives
have blown across the landscape.
We sit in the garden and form words.
Language melts in the sunlight
like an ice-cube in a clear glass.
Reality rides off on a child's bike.
Unfortunately we have to read poems.
English poets before us.
They grow metaphors in greenhouses trustingly.
They close the structure with a zipper.
Life is a dash
says a child
whose red hair's aflame.
And one moment later he hides in the pencil case
of tiny Hay-on-Wye.
In revenge I write a commissioned poem
for one hundred and fifty pounds.
I lease out my past for twenty minutes

to the assembled audience.
The breaking glass of applause.
I try to poison myself with truth
calls out one inspired poet.
An interview with Menna Elfyn.
Feminist lunch. Exchange of addresses.
My face slammed
in a camera's frames.
The rustle of Kodak film rewinding.
The darkroom's pools. We bathe in developing fluid.
Immobile towns of smiles.
Brenda Walker   (at night we sign a contract
in a London restaurant)   rises
on wings of typescripts.
Prawns' pink bodies. Warwick University.
Donald Pirie's Glasgow. Kitchen conversations
with the buzzing double-bass of food processors.
We sit in an aquarium room
and admire the prospect of utopia.
I employ imagination for a few seconds.
A sketch of air before we go.
In the Botanic Hotel a family of Italian Scots
Mr. and Mrs. Soldani
serve me soft-boiled eggs.

I leave behind for other words
Calton Hill   the extinct volcano
Mary Stuart's bedrooms with her lovers' ghosts
Jan van Eyck's portrait of 'The Arnolfini Marriage'.

I touch down on the continent's embittered province.
I throw out anchors.
I will stop here
for a few more years.

(1991)

Acknowledgements

The poems in this collection have been taken from the following
Polish editions:

Wiersze (Poems)
Czytelnik, Warsaw, 1967
Drugi zbiór wierszy (Second Collection of Poems)
Czytelnik, Warsaw, 1970
Trzeci zbiór wierszy (Third Collection of Poems)
Czytelnik, Warsaw, 1972
Czwarty zbiór wierszy (Fourth Collection of Poems)
Czytelnik, Warsaw, 1974
Piąty zbiór wierszy (Fifth Collection of Poems)
Czytelnik, Warsaw, 1979
Dom śpokojnej mlodości (The House of Quiet Youth)
Wydawnictwo Literackie, Kraków, 1978
Żywa śmierć (Living Death)
Wydawnictwo Literackie, Kraków, 1979
Nie o śmierć tutaj chodzi, lecz o biały kordonek
(I Don't Mean Death Here, But a White Piece of Thread)
Wydawnictwo Literackie, Kraków, 1982
Przechowalnia ciemności (The Storeroom of Darkness)
Independent Poets' & Artists' Publishing House, Warsaw, 1985
Utwory wybrane (Selected Poems)
Wydawnictwo Literackie, Kraków, 1986
Strefa ograniczonego postoju (The Short-stay Parking Zone)
Czytelnik, Warsaw, 1990